REAL ABILITIES — THE OMNIBUS

CREATED BY
NAVA R. SILTON, PH.D.

ILLUSTRATED BY
CHRISTOPHER GOMEZ

TABLE OF CONTENTS

PART 1

PART 2

REAL ABILITIES

CREATED BY NAVA R. SILTON, PhD

ILLUSTRATOR: CHRISTOPHER GOMEZ

MEET THE  REAL ABILITIES TEAM!

UNO

RJ

SEYMOUR

EZRA

MELODY

Realabilities "THE REAL GOAL"

CREATED BY NAVA SILTON
LEAD AUTHOR: RACHEL HOUT
CONTRIBUTING AUTHORS: SENADA ARUCEVIC AND NAVA SILTON
ILLUSTRATOR: CHRISTOPHER GOMEZ
ANIMATION DESIGN: KEENON FERRELL AND ALEX TORRES
RESEARCH TEAM: SENADA ARUCEVIC, REBECCA RUCHLIN, AND
VANESSA NORKUS

ALRIGHT KIDS, GATHER AROUND

EZRA AND GREG WILL BE CAPTAINS...

...FOR TODAY'S GAME OF *SOCCER*

YAAAAY!

AWWWW!

OK EZRA, PICK YOUR FIRST PLAYER

HMMM...

...I'LL PICK JOEY

C'MON GREG PICK YOUR NEXT PLAYER

I DON'T *WANT* ANY OF THOSE CLOWNS!

3

4

8

LATER

11

12

REAL ABILITIES
CREATED BY NAVA R. SILTON, PhD
ILLUSTRATOR: CHRISTOPHER GOMEZ

MEET THE REAL ABILITIES TEAM!

UNO

RJ

SEYMOUR

EZRA

MELODY

ADDY

Realabilities " ANTSY ADDY "

CREATED BY NAVA SILTON
LEAD AUTHOR: SENADA ARUCEVIC
CONTRIBUTING AUTHORS: SENADA ARUCEVIC AND NAVA SILTON
ILLUSTRATOR: CHRISTOPHER GOMEZ
ANIMATION DESIGN: KEENON FERRELL AND ALEX TORRES
RESEARCH TEAM: SENADA ARUCEVIC, REBECCA RUCHLIN, AND VANESSA NORKUS

HEE HEE HEE HEE

...SO WEIRD...

...LOSER...

...HAHA...

HEE HEE HEE HEE

EZRA'S GOT IT GOIN' ON! HE'S DOING GREAT!

SOMETHING TELLS ME HE'S GOING TO WIN.

EZRA WILL WIN, WIN, WIN!

THERE'S ALWAYS UPSETTING THAT DUDE...

ALWAYS UPSET

AND THOSE GUYS

...SUCH A WEIRDO

YEAH, TOTALLY

I SAY WE CHECK OUT WHAT'S COOKING OVER THERE WITH MY NEW GADGET!

WOAH WHATS THAT, MELODY?

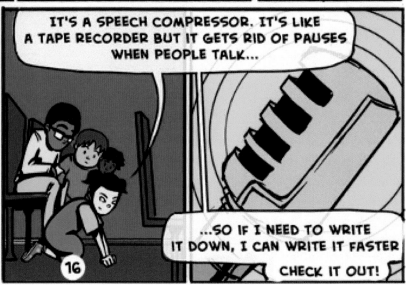

IT'S A SPEECH COMPRESSOR. IT'S LIKE A TAPE RECORDER BUT IT GETS RID OF PAUSES WHEN PEOPLE TALK...

...SO IF I NEED TO WRITE IT DOWN, I CAN WRITE IT FASTER

CHECK IT OUT!

16

19

I THINK WE SHOULD ALL ASK YOU HOW TO SPELL A WORD FROM...

...THIS UH... LARGE SET OF FLASHCARDS

I CAN HELP YOU SOUND OUT THE WORDS AND LEARN THE SYLLABLES

OR MAYBE LOOKING AT THE WORD AND JUST REMEMBERING HOW THEY ARE SPELLED IS BEST

ADDY'S HERE!

HEY GUYS! HOW'S THE STUDYING GOING?

UH... IT'S BEEN MORE BRAINSTORMING ABOUT HOW I SHOULD STUDY AND LESS STUDYING

AH HA, I SEE. SO YOU GUYS ARE HAVING A BIT OF A **BRAIN FART**?

BRAIN FART!!!

20

WHAT'S A **BRAIN FART**?

IT'S LIKE WHEN YOU'RE TRYING TO USE YOUR BRAIN BUT INSTEAD OF THOUGHTS COMING OUT, GAS COMES OUT. GAS IS NOTHING – NO THOUGHTS, JUST GAS!

THAT'S THE PERFECT TERM FOR WHAT I'M GOING THROUGH RIGHT NOW

I GET LOTS OF BRAIN BLOCKS BECAUSE OF MY ADHD. I THINK THAT'S WHY I HAVE THESE **OUTBURSTS** AND CAN GET REALLY LOUD AND PROBABLY OVERLY EXCITED SOMETIMES. I HAVE A CRAZY AMOUNT OF **ENERGY!!**

MY BRAIN BLOCKS. YOU WITH ADHD, ME WITH AUTISM

WELL, I HAVE LOW VISION, BUT WHAT'S ADHD?

KNOCK

I THINK IT'S SOMETHING ABOUT HOW LONG I CAN PAY ATTENTION, WHICH ISN'T VERY LONG!

I HAVE A PHYSICAL DISABILITY, SO I RIDE IN THIS EVERYDAY...

I'M DEAF WE ALL HAVE SOMETHING IN COMMON

21

EZRA, I THINK IT WOULD HELP IF YOU WERE CREATIVE IN HOW YOU SPELL THE WORDS. USE SENTENCES TO HELP YOU SPELL THEM OUT – WE CAN ALL THINK ABOUT COOL SENTENCES FOR EACH **WORD**!

I'M A LITTLE CONFUSED

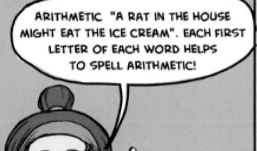
ARITHMETIC "A RAT IN THE HOUSE MIGHT EAT THE ICE CREAM". EACH FIRST LETTER OF EACH WORD HELPS TO SPELL ARITHMETIC!

THAT'S PERFECT!! IT WILL HELP ME TO AT LEAST REMEMBER THE DIFFICULT WORDS

ALL RIGHT DUDES, EVERYONE GET A STACK OF TEN CARDS AND START WRITING SENTENCES FOR 'EM!

SOUNDS LIKE A PLAN!

LADIES AND GENTLEMEN, WELCOME TO THE DISTRICT-WIDE SPELLING BEE!

EVERYONE PLEASE REMAIN SEATED AND SILENT AS WE BEGIN THE COMPETITION

GO EZRA!!!

PLEASE, HOLD YOUR APPLAUSE UNTIL THE END OF THE COMPETITION

NOW, KELLY, YOU ARE UP FIRST. PLEASE SPELL, "CAULDRON"

CAULDRON C-A-U-L-D-R-O-N CAULDRON

MAGNIFICENT M-A-G-N-I-F-UMMMM

23

COMPOUND C-O-M-P-O-U-N-D COMPOUND

UMM, COULD YOU USE IT IN A SENTENCE?

REAL ABILITIES

CREATED BY NAVA R. SILTON, Ph.D

ILLUSTRATOR: CHRISTOPHER GOMEZ

MEET THE REAL ABILITIES TEAM!

UNO

RJ

SEYMOUR

EZRA

MELODY

Realabilities "PRINCIPESSA"

CREATED BY NAVA SILTON
LEAD AUTHOR: SENADA ARUCEVIC
CONTRIBUTING AUTHORS: SENADA ARUCEVIC AND NAVA SILTON
ILLUSTRATOR: CHRISTOPHER GOMEZ
ANIMATION DESIGN: KEENON FERRELL AND ALEX TORRES
RESEARCH TEAM: SENADA ARUCEVIC, REBECCA RUCHLIN, AND VANESSA NORKUS
© 2013 NAVA R. SILTON, PH. D

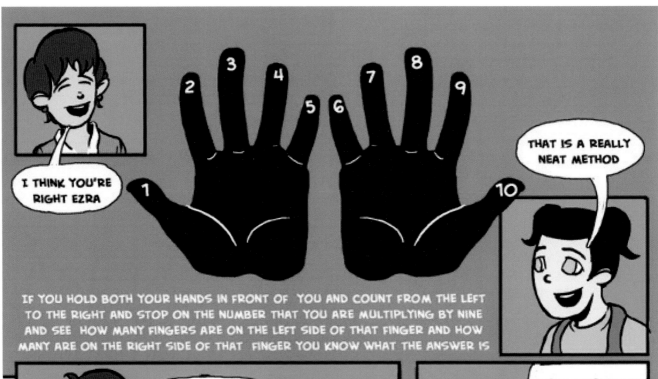

I THINK YOU'RE RIGHT EZRA

THAT IS A REALLY NEAT METHOD

IF YOU HOLD BOTH YOUR HANDS IN FRONT OF YOU AND COUNT FROM THE LEFT TO THE RIGHT AND STOP ON THE NUMBER THAT YOU ARE MULTIPLYING BY NINE AND SEE HOW MANY FINGERS ARE ON THE LEFT SIDE OF THAT FINGER AND HOW MANY ARE ON THE RIGHT SIDE OF THAT FINGER YOU KNOW WHAT THE ANSWER IS

WHAT A BEAUTIFUL ACCENT MONA. WHERE ARE YOU FROM?

ITALY

YES, NOW LET'S--

HELLO, I'M MONA, I'M A NEW STUDENT

HA HA HA HA

28

HOW WONDERFUL! WE'RE HAPPY TO HAVE YOU. YOU CAN SIT NEXT TO UNO

30

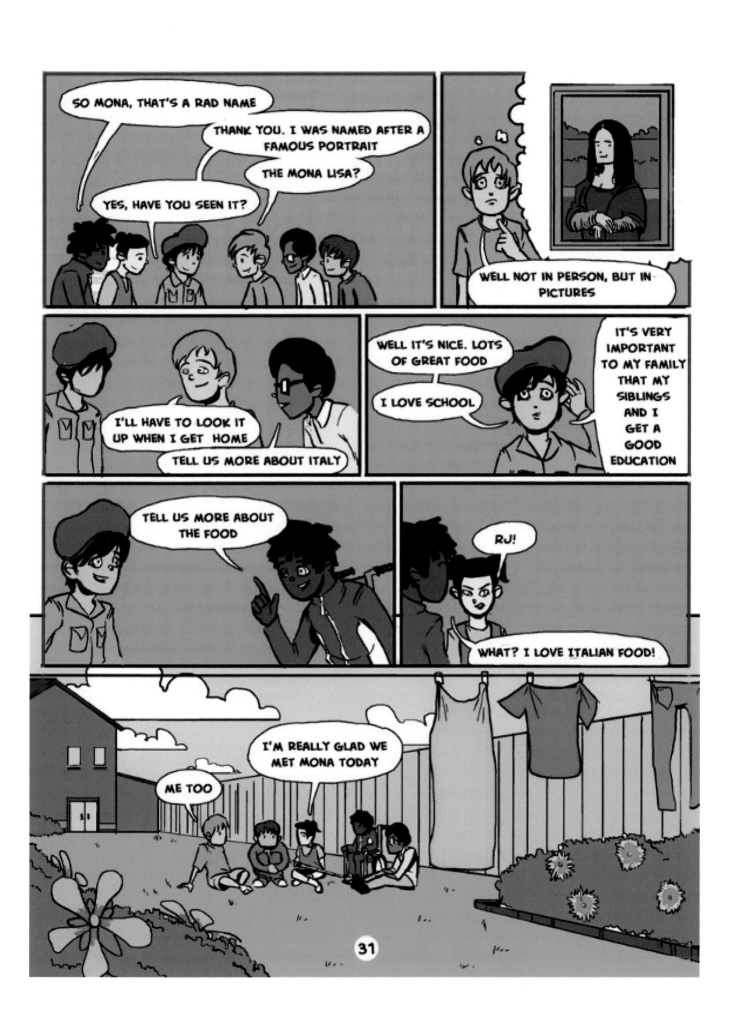

I HOPE SHE INVITES US OVER FOR A HOMEMADE ITALIAN MEAL.

RJ!

YOU GUYS CAN'T PRETEND LIKE THAT DOESN'T SOUND DELICIOUS

IT WAS INTERESTING TO HEAR HER ACCENT, IT'S SO UNIQUE

I KNOW I WISH WE COULD GET OTHER PEOPLE, LIKE JESSIE AND LYNN TO UNDERSTAND THAT JUST BECAUSE SHE SPEAKS DIFFERENTLY, DOESN'T MEAN SHE'S WEIRD

MAYBE THERE IS

WHAT ARE YOU THINKING SEYMOUR?

I CAN SEE US AT THE SCHOOL ASSEMBLY THIS WEEK

DOING WHAT DUDE?

WE'RE ALL EXPLAINING OUR CULTURES TO THE SCHOOL

LIKE A HERITAGE FESTIVAL?

YEAH WERE PEOPLE INTERESTED?

YEAH, ESPECIALLY IN MONA'S CULTURE

YEAH, LET'S HAVE A HERITAGE FESTIVAL. WE CAN ALL TALK ABOUT WHERE OUR FAMILIES COME FROM

DO IT!

MY GRANDMA CAN DRIVE US TO THE STORE TO GET SUPPLIES!

LET'S GO TEAM!

LATER THAT WEEK AT THE CULTURE FESTIVAL

UNO IS LATINO. AT HOME, OUR FAMILY SPEAKS SPANISH. UNO IS GOING TO TELL YOU A FEW SPANISH WORDS

GRACIAS

THAT MEANS THANK YOU

BUENOS DIAS

THAT MEANS GOOD DAY. UNO ALSO WANTED TO SHOW YOU WHAT WE DO TO CELEBRATE HIS FAVORITE LATIN HOLIDAY. DIA DE LOS MUERTOS. THAT MEANS "DAY OF THE DEAD." IT'S LIKE HALLOWEEN, BUT WE BELIEVE THAT THE SPIRITS OF OUR DECEASED ANCESTORS COME OUT TO CELEBRATE WITH THE LIVING

34

35

REAL ABILITIES

CREATED BY NAVA R. SILTON Ph.D
ILLUSTRATOR: CHRISTOPHER GOMEZ

MEET THE REAL ABILITIES TEAM!

UNO

RJ

SEYMOUR

EZRA

MELODY

ADDY

Realabilities   "Seemore Signs"

Created by: Nava R. Silton
Lead Authors: Rachel Hout, Senada Arucevic &
Nava Silton
Illustrator: Christopher Gomez
Animation Design: Mike Scanlon and
Christopher Gomez

39.

41

43

44

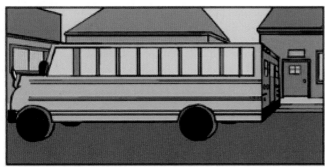
HEY SEYMOUR

HEY!

YOU OKAY SEYMOUR?

YEAH, SURE...

UMM, JUST NERVOUS ABOUT MY PRESENTATION

DO GREAT!

YOU'LL DO GREAT SEYMOUR! YOU TOO EZRA!

EZRA, PLEASE TELL THE CLASS WHO YOU BELIEVE HAS CONTRIBUTED GREATLY TO SOCIETY.

SEYMOUR, YOU'RE IN THE WINGS!

WHENEVER YOU'RE READY EZRA

GOLDA MEIR WAS THE FOURTH PRIME MINISTER OF ISRAEL

SHE WAS ISRAEL'S FIRST FEMALE PRIME MINISTER AND THE THIRD WOMAN IN THE WORLD TO HOLD SUCH AN OFFICE

SHE WAS CALLED THE "IRON LADY" OF ISRAELI POLITICS

THANK YOU EZRA.

SEYMOUR, YOU'RE UP NEXT!

THANK YOU, MR. STEWART. SORRY, I'M NERVOUS.

START WHEN YOU'RE READY, SEYMOUR!

WELL, FIRST I WAS GOING TO SPEAK ABOUT THOM..AS EDI..SON, WHO WAS A FAM...OUS INVENT..OR, WHO BECAME DEAF AS A CHILD DUE TO SCARLET FEVER.

THEN I WAS GOING TO DO MAR..LEE MAT..LIN, WHO IS A FAMOUS ACT...RESS WHO USES AMERICAN SIGN LANGUAGE (ASL)

OMG, JUST SAY WHO YOU ARE GOING TO TALK ABOUT!

SERIOUSLY!

BUT THEN I DECIDED TO TALK ABOUT ONE OF THE MOST AMAZING GIRLS I HAVE EVER MET. SHE'S BRIGHT, FUNNY, BEAUTIFUL AND USES SIGN LANGUAGE TO COMMUNICATE WITH HER DEAF COMMUNITY

SHE IS THE QUICKEST AND BEST SIGNER I HAVE EVER SEEN. MET. AND HER NAME IS...

AHEM...

EVERYONE, I'D LIKE YOU TO MEET...

...KELSEY GABOR

HELLO!

WELCOME KELSEY!

HI

THANKS

I'M HAPPY

I'M HAPPY I COULD

YOU

COULD COME

BE HERE

48

MEET THE **REAL ABILITIES**

TEAM!

UNO

RJ

SEYMOUR

EZRA

MELODY

ADDY

REALABILITIES "RJ'S ROCKET"

Created by: Nava R. Silton
Lead Authors: Rachel Hout, Senada Arucevic &
Nava Silton
Illustrator: Christopher Gomez
Animation Design: Mike Scanlon and
Christopher Gomez
©2015 NAVA R. SILTON, PH. D

RJ...
RJ...
RJ...
RJ...

GOOD MORNING!

GOOD MORNING MA!

I HAD A GREAT DREAM

ABOUT WHAT?

MY BOTTLE ROCKET! I'M WORKIN' ON IT TODAY!

SOUNDS GOOD, BUT BREAKFAST FIRST LET'S GET YOU UP

HMM...

...UHHHH...

ALRIGHT, JUST FOCUS

OH NO! THE GLUE!

GOTTA FIND A TOWEL!

HEY RJ!

UHH, HEY GUYS. WHATCHYA DOING HERE?

HELP. HERE TO HELP!

WE KNOW THE BOTTLE ROCKET COMPETITION IS COMING UP

AND WE WANT TO HELP YOU PLAN IT.

THANKS, BUT I THINK I CAN HANDLE IT ON MY OWN.

GLUE SPILLED!

THANKS UNO

MY BROTHER MADE A BOTTLE ROCKET ONCE--

COME ON GUYS! THIS IS A PIECE OF CAKE

PIECE OF CAKE? WHERE?

IT'S JUST AN EXPRESSION UNO

RJ, WE'RE HERE IF YOU NEED US

THANKS C. I JUST WANNA WIN THIS THING ON MY OWN, YA KNOW?

TOTALLY

JUST HOLLER IF YOU CHANGE YOUR MIND AND NEED HELP

WILL DO DUDES! THANKS

UGH...

WE SHOULD'VE HELPED, HELPED

I WANTED TO HELP TOO UNO,

BUT RJ REALLY WANTED TO DO IT ON HIS OWN

I LIKE DOING THINGS ON MY OWN

ME TOO!

WAIT! I HAVE A PLAN

PSST... PSST PSST...

PEW PEW BAM

KNOCK KNOCK

IUSE
ESUME
QUIT

YOU SURE KNOW HOW TO SURPRISE A GUY!

WE THOUGHT WE WOULD COME OVER TO SEE THE ROCKET?

I GAVE UP ON THAT

RJ, YOU KNOW IT'S OKAY TO ASK FOR HELP

I ASK!

I ALWAYS ASK UNO TO HELP ME WITH MY MATH HOMEWORK

HELP WITH MATH HOMEWORK!

NO ONE WOULD THINK ANY LESS OF YOU IF YOU ASKED FOR HELP. WE'D LOVE TO HELP

REALLY DUDES?

OF COURSE! WE ALWAYS WANT TO HELP EACH OTHER AND ANYONE WHO NEEDS IT.

YOU'D REALLY BE GAME TO HELP ME WITH MY ROCKET? IT'S TOUGH TO DO ON MY OWN

GOOD THING I ALREADY HAVE A PLAN...

ALRIGHT, LET'S GET TO WORK

LET'S GET THIS ROCKET BACK INTO SHAPE!

AWESOME IDEAS, UNO!

THE ROCKET WILL DEFINITELY FLY WITH THESE PLANS!

FLY!

HMMM...

I THINK I'VE COME UP WITH AN AWESOME COLOR SCHEME

ALSO, I'VE INSTALLED A NICE MUSICAL SURPRISE WHEN IT LAUNCHES

ALRIGHT RJ, THIS IS THE LAST PIECE I NEED TO CUT...

...AND THERE! I THINK WE'RE DONE SON!

THANKS EVERYONE THE ROCKET LOOKS GREAT!

57

A FIERCE COMPETITION IS BREWING BETWEEN OUR YOUNG ROCKETEERS!

AND WITH ALL ROCKETS LAUNCHED... IT IS TIME TO ANNOUNCE THE WINNER!

IN THIRD PLACE, WE HAVE REBECCA!

IN SECOND, RJ!

AND IN FIRST PLACE...

...NEIL!!!

CELEBRATION?

DEFINITELY, UNO, BBQ AT OUR PLACE. I ALREADY ASKED ALL OF YOUR PARENTS, AND THEY'LL PICK YOU UP TONIGHT

DAD, CAN I INVITE SOME OF THE OTHER KIDS?

SURE

59

HEY REBECCA!

WANNA COME TO MY HOUSE TO CELEBRATE?

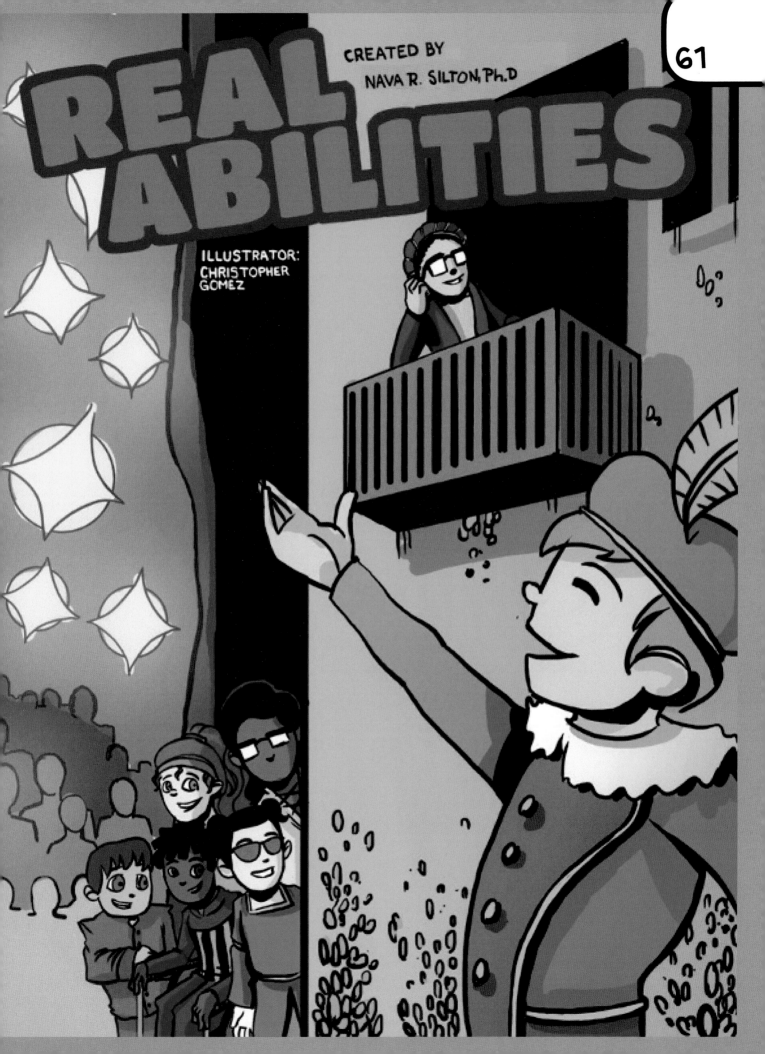

MEET THE REAL ABILITIES TEAM!

UNO

RJ

SEYMOUR

EZRA

MELODY

ADDY

Realabilities "Play Nice"

Created by: Nava R. Silton
Lead Authors: Rachel Hout, Senada Arucevic & Jennifer Santamaria
Illustrator: Christopher Gomez
Animation Design: Keenon Ferrell & Alex Torres
Research Team: Senada Arucevic, Rebecca Ruchlin, Alicia Ferris
Marymount Manhattan College

63

OMG LET THE UNFORTUNATE AUDITIONS CONTINUE. LOOK WHOSE UP NEXT.

NERD ALERT! NERD ALERT!

THOSE ARE THE THICKEST, GEEKIEST GLASSES I'VE EVER SEEN

THAT'S ENOUGH GIRLS. GO AHEAD, ALEXA

MISS B., I'M SORRY, I DIDN'T THINK I'D BE THIS NERVOUS

ALEXA, TAKE A DEEP BREATH. START WHEN YOU'RE READY

GEEEEEZ!!!

GIRLS, I MEAN IT! ALEXA, COME ON BACK!

HOUSTON, WE HAVE A PROBLEM

IT'S LIZZY AND CINDY...THEY BULLIED ALEXA AT HER AUDITION AND SHE RAN OFF

HEY MEL, WHAT'S THE REAL DEAL?

LOOK...

SHE EVEN LEFT HER GLASSES

I CAN GET THEM BACK TO HER LICKITY-SPLIT!

SEE!

YES! SHE'S RUNNING THROUGH THE SCHOOL YARD...

AND SHE'S HEADING... TOWARDS THE SWINGS!

UNO, HOW QUICKLY CAN WE GET THERE?

3 MINUTES. 43 SECONDS

WE NEED TO MAKE SURE SHE GETS ANOTHER CHANCE TO AUDITION

65

MELODY, YOU'RE UP!

THANK YOU MISS B, BUT I'M GOING TO SIT THIS ONE OUT.

THANKS, BUT...

BUT WE HAVE NO TIME!

UNO CALCULATED HOW LONG ALEXA HAS BEEN GONE SO FAR

5 MINUTES, 32 SECONDS

SO, GO SING YOUR HEART OUT MELODY!

MISS B, CAN I MAKE A DEAL WITH YOU?

YES, MELODY

IF YOU PROMISE ME THAT ALEXA CAN TRY OUT AGAIN ON FRIDAY, THEN I WILL TRY OUT TODAY

SURE THING

♪ WHEN YOU PUT IN ALL YOUR EFFORT AND YOU STUDIED FOR THE TEST YOU CAN BE PROUD. SO LONG AS YOU TRIED YOUR BEST! ♪

WE HAVE TO HURRY GUYS!

COME ON GUYS, I BET I CAN GET THERE FIRST

15.34 MILES AN HOUR

ARE YOU OK ALEXA?

ALEXA!

I KNEW IT WAS A MISTAKE TO TRY OUT. IT WAS AWFUL. I PRACTICALLY GOT BOOED OFF STAGE

I'M SO EMBARRASSED AND I NEVER WANT TO SING AGAIN.

LIZZIE AND CINDY ARE BIG BULLIES!

THEY LIKE TO PUT OTHER PEOPLE DOWN SO THAT THEY CAN FEEL BETTER ABOUT THEMSELVES

WHAT'S THE POINT? I BLEW THE AUDITION. I'LL NEVER GET ANOTHER CHANCE.

MISS B ALREADY SAID YOU'D GET ANOTHER CHANCE

JUST LET US HELP YOU

ALRIGHT ALEXA...

YOU CAN START SINGING WHENEVER YOU WANT

THANKS MELODY

LALALA LALA...

BLAAAAAHHHHH...!

TCH

BOOM BOOM

OK FOCUS...

♪ YOU HAVE GOT TO TRY, TRY, TRY, YOUR BEST. YOU HAVE TO GIVE IT ALL AND FORGET ABOUT ALL THE REST ♪

THAT SOUNDS GREAT

♪ THANK YOU GUYS... ALL OF YOU... ♪

70

NO PROBLEM

YOU'RE GONNA DO GREAT ALEXA

THANK YOU CINDY. ALEXA, YOU'RE UP NEXT...

...YOU'LL BE TRYING OUT FOR THE SUPPORTING LEAD

THE NEXT DAY AT THE AUDITORIUM

ALEXA, YOU'VE GOT THIS! SHOW THEM YOUR STUFF!

YOU HAVE GOT TO TR--TR--TRY...

MAY I START ONE MORE TIME?

TAKE YOUR TIME ALEXA

CINDY AND LIZZIE, ONCE MORE AND YOU'RE OUT!

EASY, ADDY LET'S FOCUS ON ALEXA

OHHH, I OUGHT TO SHOW THEM A THING OR TWO...

OKAY FOCUS... JUST FOCUS ON YOUR SONG

71

♪ YOU HAVE GOT TO TRY, TRY, TRY, YOUR BEST. YOU HAVE TO GIVE IT ALL AND FORGET ABOUT ALL THE REST. WHEN YOU PUT IN ALL YOUR EFFORT AND YOU STUDIED FOR THE TEST, ♪

♪ YOU CAN BE PROUD. SO LONG AS YOU TRIED YOUR BEST! ♪

WOAH..

CONGRATULATIONS ALEXA! YOU WILL BE OUR SUPPORTING LEAD!

THANK YOU, THANK YOU MISS B AND THE WHOLE REALABILITIES TEAM!

CONGRATULATIONS

I THINK SOME SMOOTHIES ARE IN ORDER

HEY ALEXA, I MUST ADMIT, YOU REALLY ROCKED THAT STAGE

YEAH

THANKS WANNA COME AND GET SOME SMOOTHIES?

SUCCESS TEAM!

72

REAL ABILITIES

CREATED BY NAVA R. SILTON, Ph.D

ILLUSTRATOR: CHRISTOPHER GOMEZ

MEET THE REAL ABILITIES TEAM!

UNO

RJ

SEYMOUR

EZRA

MELODY

ADDY

Realabilities "Math Mania"

Created by: Nava R. Silton
Lead Author: Jordan Geary
Illustrator: Christopher Gomez
Animation Design: Christopher Gomez and
Michael Scanlon
Research Team: Alicia Ferris, A. Kristina Keyser,
Carol Wagner, Alexis Wilson, Kathryn Rouse, Michael Corning,
& Michael Rojas

74

75

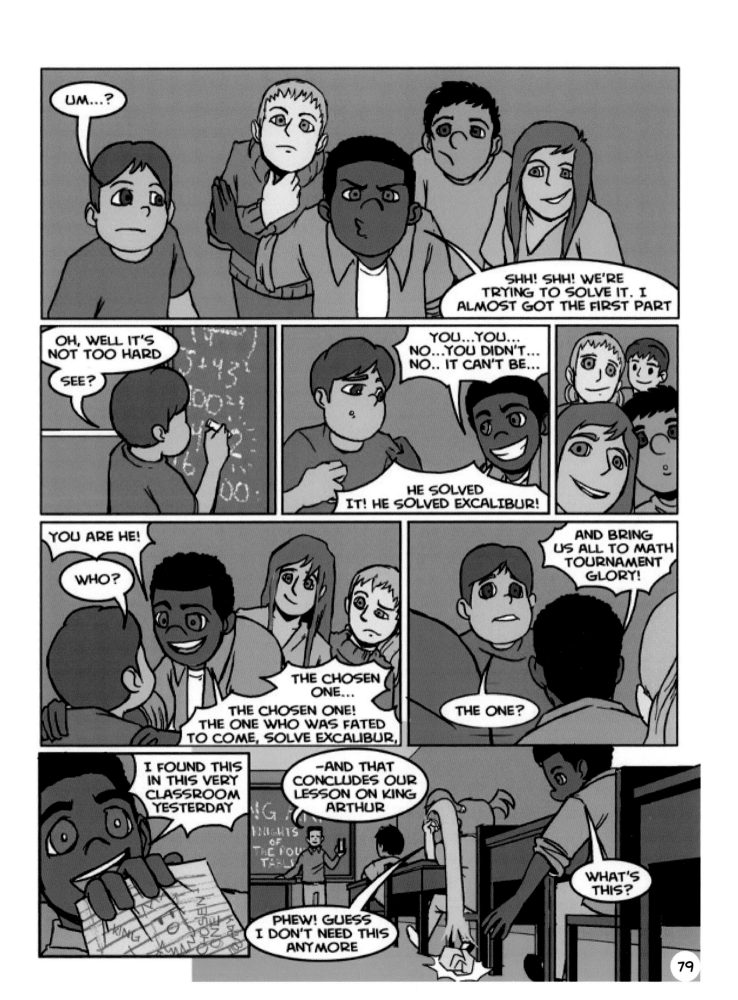

-BUT IT ALSO SAYS, "CHOSEN ONE" ON IT

SO?!

ONE? UNO? YOUR NAME IS ONE?

YOU ARE THE CHOSEN ONE! IT'S RIGHT THERE IN YOUR NAME!

ALL HAIL UNO! ALL HAIL THE CHOSEN ONE!

OH NO!

ALL HAIL UNO! ALL HAIL THE CHOSEN ONE!

ADDY? MELODY? SEYMOUR? EZRA? WHAT ARE YOU DOING?

WE'RE READYING OURSELVES FOR OUR BEAUTIFUL RED PRIZE BIKE.

THE BEST WAY TO PREPARE IS BY RIDING IMAGINARY BIKES

EVEN TINY IS INTO IT!

I'M GLAD YOU ARE HAVING FUN...

...BUT I'M NOT COMPETING IN THE MATH TOURNAMENT

WHAT?!

WHAT? BUT —BUT YOU HAVE TO!

NO I DON'T

BUT YOU LIKE MATH RIGHT?

YES

AND YOU LIKE NEW MENTAL CHALLENGES, RIGHT?

YES

AND THIS IS BOTH!

YES, BUT THIS IS IN FRONT OF OTHER PEOPLE WITH LOTS OF SCARY LIGHTS

WISE AS ALWAYS, MELODY

YEAH, UNO, ANY OF THE PRESSURE YOU ARE FEELING IS PRESSURE FROM YOURSELF

WE LOVE YOU, BUDDY

ANYHOO, WE'RE OFF TO THE PARK.

WANT TO JOIN?

NO, I HAVE SOME-WHERE I HAVE TO BE

THIS DOOR NEEDS FIXING!

BANG!

IT'S THE CHOSEN ONE!

DO I HAVE TO STAND IN FRONT OF A BIG AUDIENCE?

NO, WE CAN STAND IN FRONT OF YOU TO BLOCK YOU, IF YOU'D LIKE

WHY?

AND DO I HAVE TO ANSWER THE QUESTIONS DIRECTLY AT THIS EVENT?

NO, YOU CAN WHISPER THEM TO US

AND DO I HAVE TO DO THAT ANNOYING "HISS" THING YOU ALL DO?

NAH, IT'S COOL

I'M IN

83

REAL ABILITIES

ILLUSTRATOR: CHRISTOPHER GOMEZ

CREATED BY NAVA R. SILTON, Ph.D

MEET THE REAL ABILITIES

TEAM!

UNO

RJ

SEYMOUR

EZRA

MELODY

ADDY

and Special Guest: Dberek

Realabilities
"Chemistry Craze"

Created by Nava R. Silton, Ph.D.
Lead Authors: Nava Silton & Rachel Hout
Contributing Authors: Hannah Peikes and Senada Arucevic
Illustrator: Christopher Gomez
Animation Design: Christopher Gomez and Michael Scanlon
Research Team: Nava R. Silton, Hannah Peikes,
Carol Wagner & Alicia Ferris

90

LOOK SAM, LITTLE DBEREK IS TRYING TO HIDE HIS LITTLE STAIN, HAHA!

GREG, THIS IS YOUR LAST WARNING

DBEREK, WHY DON'T YOU WORK OVER HERE?

YOU CAN WORK ON YOUR OWN, IF YOU WISH

HOUSTON, PROBLEM!

COMPLETED! IT LOOKS LIKE A SLIGHTLY BUBBLY, EFFERVESCENT RESULT. I AM NOW EAGER TO UTILIZE AGENT d.

HMM...

91

HOUSTON, ENTER...

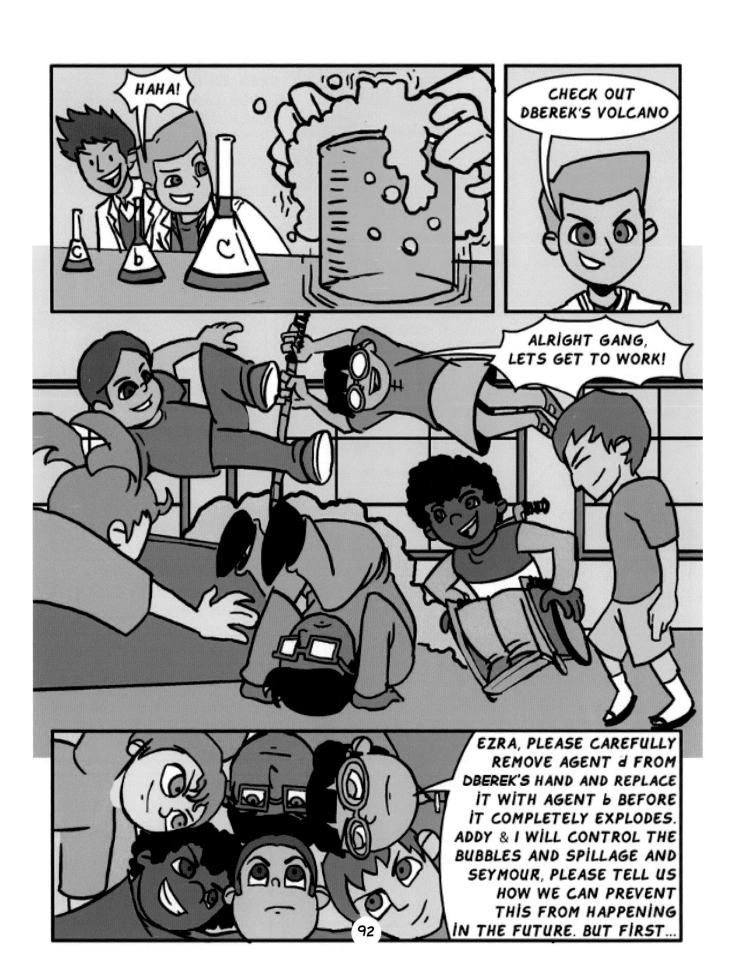

MY VISION REVEALS THAT DBEREK HAS DYSLEXIA: HE MISTOOK THE LETTER b FOR THE LETTER d. DYSLEXIA MAKES IT DIFFICULT TO READ SOMETIMES, SINCE LETTERS AND WORDS CAN GET JUMBLED, SCRAMBLED OR MIXED UP WE NEED TO CREATE A BETTER WAY TO LABEL THESE BOTTLES

WELL WE HAVE NO TIME TO FIGURE THAT OUT,

WE GOTTA GO!

ADDY! NOT OUT THE WINDOW! WE'RE IN THIS CLASS!

OH, RIGHT

WAIT, WHAT WERE YOU TALKING ABOUT, GREG? WHAT VOLCANO?

HUH?

HMM...

OH, HERE'S THE RIGHT CHEMICAL

⇒SNEAK⇐

94

95

REAL ABILITIES

ILLUSTRATOR: CHRISTOPHER GOMEZ

CREATED BY NAVA R. SILTON, Ph.D

MEET THE REAL ABILITIES TEAM!

UNO

RJ

SEYMOUR

EZRA

MELODY

ADDY

and Special Guest: Lexxy

Realabilities "Food Fight"

Created by Nava R. Silton, Ph.D.
Lead Authors: Nava Silton & Rachel Hout
Contributing Authors: Hannah Peikes and Senada Arucevic
Illustrator: Christopher Gomez
Animation Design: Christopher Gomez and Michael Scanlon
Research Team: Nava R. Silton, Hannah Peikes,
Carol Wagner & Alicia Ferris

100

101

FOOD FIGHT

3PLAT!

MELODY, DUCK! UNO, TO YOUR LEFT!

THANKS, SEYMOUR!

WHOAH!! FOOD FIGHT!

WOW, NICE PERCEPTUAL SKILLS!

STOOOOOPPPPPP THIS MADNESS!!!!

WHO STARTED THIS?! THE CULPRIT BETTER COME FOWARD!

IF NOT THERE WILL BE SOME SERIOUS CONSEQUENCES.

I EXPECT THIS PLACE TO BE SPOTLESS BY THE END OF LUNCH.

WHO DID DO IT?

WHO DID DO IT?

DUDE, SEYMOUR, WHAT'S UP? YOU LOOK SO SERIOUS BRO

I KNOW WHO STARTED THE FIGHT

I SPOTTED HIM EYEING THE CAFETERIA MENU

ALL OF A SUDDEN HE STOOD UP AND THREW FOOD

LET'S GO SEE WHAT HIS DEAL IS?

HEY STANLEY

OH, HEY GUYS

YOU STARTED THE FIGHT

WHAT?!

UNO MEANS—

EXACTLY WHAT HE SAID. WHY DID YOU DO IT MAN?

WE WON'T TELL THE PRINCIPAL, WE JUST WANT TO KNOW WHY YOU STARTED THE FIGHT

I WAS JUST FRUSTRATED

ABOUT WHAT?

THIS STUPID CAFETERIA AND THIS STUPID FOOD!

YO' DON'T DISH ON THE FOOD MAN. I LOVE THIS FOOD!

THAT'S BECAUSE YOU DON'T HAVE ALLERGIES

ALLERGIES?

YEAH, I'M ALLERGIC TO GLUTEN, CASEIN AND NUTS. IT LIMITS SO MUCH OF WHAT I CAN EAT

WHAT ARE GLUTEN AND CASEIN?

GLUTEN IS A PROTEIN COMPOSITE FOUND IN WHEAT, BARLEY, RYE, ETC.

CASEIN IS THE PROTEIN FOUND IN ALL MAMMALS' MILK

THAT'S ROUGH MAN! NO WHEAT OR MILK PRODUCTS? THAT'S ALL I EAT!

YAH, I WAS SO HUNGRY, I ATE SOME PASTA EVEN THOUGH I KNEW IT WOULD HURT MY STOMACH. IT HURT, I WAS FRUSTRATED AND THREW THE FOOD. I DIDN'T KNOW IT WOULD HIT KATE.

I HAVE A DUST ALLERGY

THERE ARE MANY COMMON ALLERGIES THAT AFFECT A LARGE PART OF THE POPULATION

SORRY, YOU'RE SO FRUSTRATED STANLEY

I GOT IT!!

FIRST, THINK COOKING ELECTIVE, MR. ROBINSON, MY FIASCO FEAST, EZRA'S GINORMOUS GOOEY MESS

AND LEXXY'S TREMENDOUS, STUPENDOUS, APPETITE-QUENCHING, DELIRIOUSLY DELICIOUS EPICUREAN DELIGHT!

I THINK ADDY'S SUGGESTING THAT WE GIVE THIS MASTER CHEF IN OUR COOKING CLASS, THE INGREDIENTS YOU CAN EAT...

HUH?

GOOD CALL ADDY!

AND SEE WHAT SHE CAN WHIP UP FOR YOU AND FOR THE OTHER STUDENTS

YOU'D DO THAT FOR ME?

STANLEY, WE'RE ON IT...

...AS SOON AS YOU MARCH YOUR FOOD FIGHT STARTER SELF OVER TO APOLOGIZE TO KATE AND TO COME CLEAN TO THE PRINCIPAL

107

YOU GOT A DEAL!

HIYA LEXXY, THE INCREDIBLE MASTERFUL, EPICUREAN CHEF OF THE SCHOOL!

HIYA ALL

WHY ARE YOU PUTTING PLASTIC ON YOUR FEET?

OH THESE ARE JUST MY ORTHOTICS. THEY HELP ME WALK, RUN AND THEY CENTER MY BODY. I USED TO HAVE HUGE BRACES LIKE SOME OF MY OTHER FRIENDS WITH DOWN SYNDROME

I JUST GOT OUT OF PHYSICAL THERAPY SO I HAVE TO PUT THESE BACK ON

I HAVE PHYSICAL THERAPY SPEECH THERAPY, TOO!

BACK TO ME!

DON'T YOU JUST LOVE SPEECH WITH SAMMY?

LEXXY, WE HAVE THE PROPOSAL OF THE CENTURY FOR YOU MY FRIEND!

BY WHEN DO WE NEED THE RECIPES AND MENU?

TOMORROW

WHAT?!

A-D-D-Y!!

WE'LL HELP!!!

IT'S OK MELODY, I'M IN! LET'S SEE WHAT WE CAN WHIP UP!

RIP!

NO MEASUREMENTS? TSP? TBSP? CUPS

NOPE!

SOMETIMES I HAVE TROUBLE READING THROUGH LONG LISTS OF INGREDIENTS OR REMEMBERING EXACT MEASUREMENTS. A LOT OF KIDS WITH DOWN SYNDROME HAVE A TOUGH TIME WITH MEMORY AND READING,

BUT I DON'T LET THAT STOP ME FROM DOING WHAT I LOVE!

CHECK OUT THIS DELICIOUS SMELLING PIZZA

NO NUTS, GLUTEN OR CASEIN. THIS SURE LOOKS DIVINE

NO WAY!! FIVE DIFFERENT NUT FREE, GLUTEN AND CASEIN-FREE CHOICES?

HA, YOU ORDERING FROM THE DIET MENU?

WHAT? THIS STUFF LOOKS A-M-A-Z-I-N-G!!

MISS HOW'D THIS HAPPEN?

THOSE KID'S ARE THE ONES TO THANK.

THEY BROUGHT IN ALL THESE GREAT RECIPE'S THIS MORNING!

HEAR, HEAR!

GOLDEN CHEF!

LEXXY, OUR GOLDEN CHEF!

MEET THE  TEAM!

UNO

RJ

SEYMOUR

EZRA

MELODY

ADDY

and Special Guests: Beat, Venn, and Tee

Realabilities
"We've Got the Beat"

Created by Nava R. Silton, Ph.D.
Lead Authors: Nava Silton & Hannah Peikes
Illustrator: Christopher Gomez
Animation Design: Christopher Gomez and Michael Scanlon
Research Team: Nava R. Silton, Hannah Peikes, Carol Wagner & Alicia Ferris

112

STUDENTS OF 4J ELEMENTARY, HAVE YOU EVER WANTED TO BE FAMOUS? HEREIN LIES A ONCE IN A LIFETIME OPPORTUNITY! OUR SCHOOL WILL BE HOLDING A MUSIC VIDEO CONTEST! ARE YOU A DANCER, A SINGER, OR PERFORMER? DO YOU HAVE A MUSICAL TALENT? WELL IF SO, THIS IS THE CONTEST FOR YOU! VIDEO ENTRIES OF YOUR MUSICAL TALENTS WILL BE DUE NEXT FRIDAY AT 3 PM SHARP IN MISS KIMMEL'S MAILBOX IN THE MAIN OFFICE. STUDENTS IN THE WINNING VIDEO WILL NOT ONLY BE FEATURED ON OUR SCHOOL WEBSITE AND ON ALL OF OUR SCHOOL TV SCREENS, BUT STUDENTS WILL HAVE AN OPPORTUNITY TO PERFORM THEIR TALENT ON DR. NAV, OUR LOCAL TALKSHOW!

113

114

UH...OH!

WOAH!

BEATRICE! YOU!

YOU SHOULD ENTER THE VIDEO CONTEST! OH PLS! OH PLS! OH PLS! IF I CAN'T BE FAMOUS, AT LEAST I CAN KNOW SOMEONE WHO IS!

CCCONTEST? FFAMOUS, NNOT FOR ME! TTHANKS ANYWAY!

BEATRICE, YOU'RE HANDS-DOWN, THE BEST HIP-HOP DANCER IN OUR DANCE CLASS!

TTTHANKS, BBBUT I'LL PPASS

LATER AT LUNCH...

WHAT'S UP WITH ADDY?

WHAT'S UP WITH ADDY?

115

116

IT JUST DOESN'T MAKE SENSE. SOMETHING'S DEFINITELY UP

OK CLASS, WHAT A WONDERFUL JOB TODAY! WE'LL END 10 MINUTES EARLY TODAY TO GIVE THOSE DELIGHTFUL VOICES A NICE REST.

REMEMBER, DRINKS WITH HONEY AND LEMON BEFORE TUESDAY'S CHORUS PERFORMANCE IN THE SCHOOL AUDI- TORIUM! CHEERS!

MELODY, IT LOOKS LIKE OUR REALABILITIES TEAM HAS A BIGGER MYSTERY TO SOLVE.

IT'S NOT JUST BEATRICE! VENN, BEATRICE AND TEE ARE NOT SINGING A SINGLE WORD

I MAY HAVE TROUBLE SEEING, BUT MY HEAR- ING'S PRETTY GOOD. THEY STAND RIGHT BEHIND ME AND I HAVEN'T HEARD ONE NOTE FROM THEM

MAYBE THEY'RE ALL SHY?

LOOKS LIKE WE HAVE OUR WORK CUT OUT FOR US

LET'S GET TO THE BOTTOM OF THIS

VENN, BEATRICE, TEE, WILL WE SEE YOU AT TUESDAY'S PERFOR -MANCE?

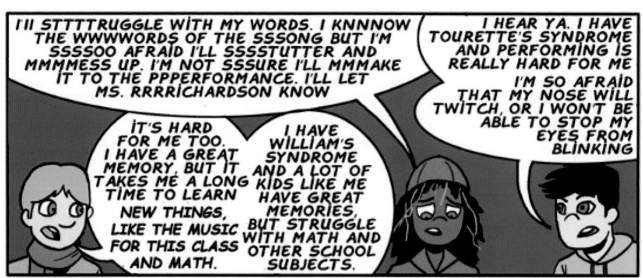

120

I HAVE TO ADMIT, I THOUGHT THE WHOLE TAPE THING WAS WEIRD...

BOOP!

...BUT I AM SERIOUSLY IMPRESSED, YOU'RE A GREAT DANCER

THANK G, WE FINALLY FOUND SOMEONE COMPETENT

THE NEXT DAY

I DON'T KNOW ABOUT THOSE OTHER WEIRDOS ON THE TAPE

YEAH, THEY'RE WHATEVER. BUT YOU!

YEAH, THOSE OTHER KIDS CAN'T HOLD A CANDLE TO YOU

DON'T WORRY ABOUT THAT NOW, BEATRICE

YEAH, YOU'RE A PART OF A GROUP WITH SOME ACTUAL TALENT NOW

LATER THAT WEEK

WONDERFUL, TALENTED STUDENTS OF 4J ELEMENTARY, OUR FINE JUDGES HAVE UNANIMOUSLY SELECTED THE WINNERS OF OUR VIDEO TALENT CONTEST. THESE INCREDIBLE PERFORMERS WILL APPEAR ON OUR WEB SITE, ON OUR SCREENS AND ON...DR. NAV!!!

YOU'VE SO GOT THIS, BEATRICE!! BEATRICE HAS THE BEAT!

THAT'S REALLY CLEVER, ADDY!

BEATRICE, CAN WE CALL YOU BEAT?

SURE I GUESS KKINDA LLIKE THAT!

THE WINNERS OF OUR CONTEST ARE...BEATRICE, ADDY, UNO, SEYMOUR, MELODY, EZRA, RJ, VENN, AND TEE!

CONGRATULATIONS!!!

121

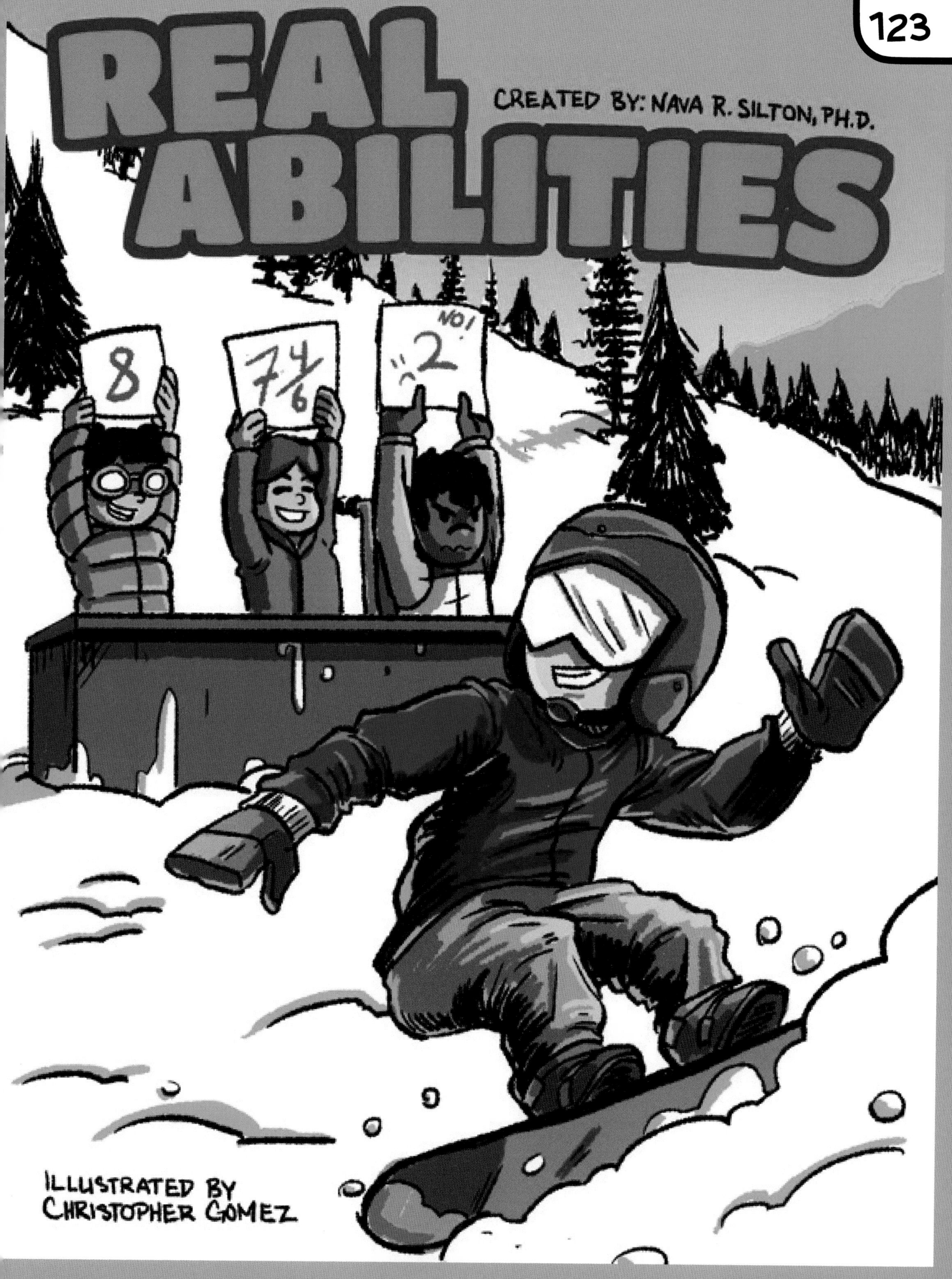
REAL ABILITIES
CREATED BY: NAVA R. SILTON, PH.D.
8
7 4/6
NO!
2
ILLUSTRATED BY
CHRISTOPHER GOMEZ

MEET THE

TEAM!

UNO

ROLLY

SEEMORE

EZRA

MELODY

ADDY

FEATURING

REALABILITIES
"HEAD FIRST"

GREG

DBEREK

VENN

CREATED BY: NAVA R. SILTON, PH.D.
LEAD AUTHORS: MICHAL RICHARDSON AND NAVA SILTON
ILLUSTRATOR: CHRISTOPHER GOMEZ
ANIMATION DESIGN: CHRISTOPHER GOMEZ AND MICHAEL SCANLON
RESEARCH TEAM: NAVA R. SILTON, PH.D., PATRICK RILEY,
EDEN JACOBSON AND MICHAL KAHAN.

SO I TOLD THE INSTRUCTOR, "ME? WEAR A HELMET? THAT'S FOR AMATEURS, DUDE."

YOU SHOULD'VE SEEN THAT FALL I TOOK—I COULD'VE BEEN A MOVIE STUNTMAN!

THE REALABILITIES TEAM RETURNS FROM WINTER BREAK...

THEY FOUND MY SNOWBOARD TWENTY FEET AWAY!

WHOOOOOA. SO THAT'S HOW YOU BROKE YOUR LEG?

YEP! I HIT MY HEAD, I GOT THIS SWEET CAST, AND I SCORED THOSE AWESOME CRUTCHES!

HEY! YOU'VE HAD YOUR TURN; GIVE SOMEONE ELSE A TRY!

CAN I SIGN YOUR CAST, GREG?

YOU? SIGN IT? CAN YOU EVEN SEE IT?

WELCOME BACK, EVERYONE! I HOPE YOU HAD AN EXCITING WINTER BREAK... IF NOT QUITE AS EXCITING AS GREG'S.

WE'RE HAVING A TEST ON FRACTIONS THIS FRIDAY, SO IT'S TIME TO START PREPARING.

UH-OH. FRACTIONS? I DEFINITELY NEED TO PRACTICE THOSE.

HA! MAYBE YOU DO. BUT I DON'T SWEAT FRACTIONS. I LEARNED THAT STUFF LAST YEAR!

WELCOME BACK, GREG! WE MISSED YOU.

FRIDAY MORNING...

SORRY I'M LATE, MS. Z. I, UH... I, UH HAD A HEADACHE THIS MORNING...

YEAH. ANYWAY, SORRY.

I... SEE. AND I HOPE YOU GOT THE HOMEWORK CINDY'S BEEN BRINGING YOU.

AW, MAN! I GOT THROUGH ALMOST ALL OF IT, AND THEN... UGH. IT MUST HAVE BEEN UNDER MY NOTEBOOK.

I CAN SEE THIS IS GOING TO BE A LONG DAY. FOR ALL OF US. BUT TAKE YOUR SEAT, GREG. YOU'RE JUST IN TIME FOR FRACTION FRIDAY! PUT AWAY THOSE BOOKS AND SHARPEN YOUR PENCILS, EVERYONE!

A TEST! RIGHT, RIGHT, THAT WAS TODAY... WELL, NO BIGGIE. THE MATH SNAKES CALL ME THE FRACTION MASTER!

IT'LL BE A PIECE OF CAKE

FLIP... AND...

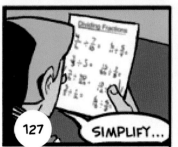

SIMPLIFY...

THANK YOU, VENN. GO ON AND GET CHANGED FOR GYM

AW, MAN. I'M LAST! I'M NEVER LAST IN MATH! AND THIS HEADACHE IS GETTING WORSE!

WELL... IF I'M LAST, I GUESS NO ONE ELSE WILL SEE...

...THESE.

TIME'S UP, GREG. I CAN'T KEEP MS. WHIFFLE WAITING ALL DAY.

ALL RIGHT, ALL RIGHT, I'LL HEAD TO GYM! HERE.

I WISH I COULD JUST STAY HOME FOREVER.

NOT LIKE I'M EVEN ALLOWED TO TAKE GYM THESE DAYS, ANYWAY.

OH, HEY, GREG! I GET TO BE JOKE MONITOR THIS WEEK, AND I'M HAVING A BALL - A SNOWBALL!

WHAT DO YOU FIND IN SCHOOL IN JANUARY CHILL-DREN!

BLAM!

OOF!!!

HEE HEE... HEY GREG

COOL NEW SHADES, MAN!

DID YOU GET THEM TO MATCH YOUR COOL NEW FRIENDS? HA!

HERE, GREG...

GIVE ME THAT!

I DON'T NEED HELP FROM YOU NERDS! I'VE GOT ENOUGH PROBLEMS ALREADY.

THIS HEADACHE WON'T GO AWAY, I COULDN'T EVEN HANDLE FRACTIONS, AND I'M NOT ALLOWED TO PLAY BALL, AND I FORGOT MY HOMEWORK, AND—

JUST BUZZ OFF, SEEMORE!

GREG, I—

AT LUNCH...

...AND HE WAS WEARING THESE THICK GLASSES!

WOW. SOMETHING MUST BE GRAVELY PROBLEMATIC HERE.

MAYBE THERE'S SOMETHING WE CAN DO TO HELP!

MEL, YOU SERIOUSLY WANT TO HELP?

JUST THIS MONDAY HE WAS RUDE TO YOU AND VENN!

AND REMEMBER CHEMISTRY CLASS IN OCTOBER? HE SABOTAGED MY WHOLE EXPERIMENT!

AND HE NEVER CHOSE ANY OF US FOR SOCCER. EVER

SEE, MEL? GREG'S BEEN EXTRA MEAN LATELY. WHY FOCUS ON HIM, WHEN WE COULD BE THINKING ABOUT FRIDAY FRENCH FRIES?

HE'S PROBABLY BEEN EXTRA MEAN BECAUSE HE HAS AN EXTRA-HUGE PROBLEM!

...WHICH MEANS WE COULD HELP HIM SOLVE IT! WE'RE GREAT AT SOLVING PROBLEMS!

LET'S MEET UP THIS WEEKEND AND DO SOME RESEARCH!

WE COULD RESEARCH WITH WAFFLES...

130

DEAL! I'M COOKING SUNDAY BRUNCH AT MY PLACE. PARTY STARTS AT 10 AM!

HE MUST HAVE HIT HIS HEAD REALLY HARD WHEN HE FELL OFF HIS SNOWBOARD.

SUNDAY BRUNCH AT RJ'S...

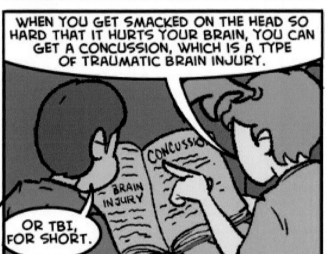

WHEN YOU GET SMACKED ON THE HEAD SO HARD THAT IT HURTS YOUR BRAIN, YOU CAN GET A CONCUSSION, WHICH IS A TYPE OF TRAUMATIC BRAIN INJURY.

OR TBI, FOR SHORT.

CONCUSSION

BRAIN INJURY

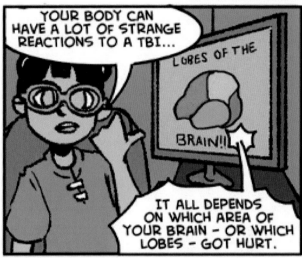

YOUR BODY CAN HAVE A LOT OF STRANGE REACTIONS TO A TBI...

LOBES OF THE

BRAIN!!

IT ALL DEPENDS ON WHICH AREA OF YOUR BRAIN - OR WHICH LOBES - GOT HURT.

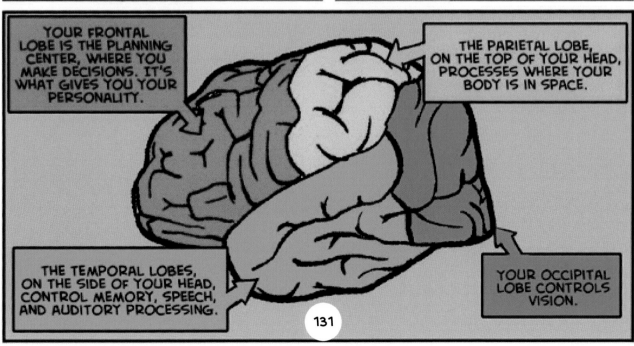

YOUR FRONTAL LOBE IS THE PLANNING CENTER, WHERE YOU MAKE DECISIONS. IT'S WHAT GIVES YOU YOUR PERSONALITY.

THE PARIETAL LOBE, ON THE TOP OF YOUR HEAD, PROCESSES WHERE YOUR BODY IS IN SPACE.

THE TEMPORAL LOBES, ON THE SIDE OF YOUR HEAD, CONTROL MEMORY, SPEECH, AND AUDITORY PROCESSING.

YOUR OCCIPITAL LOBE CONTROLS VISION.

131

GREG IS HAVING VISION PROBLEMS... AND MEMORY TROUBLES. AND HEADACHES.

SO HE MUST HAVE DAMAGE TO HIS OCCIPITAL AND TEMPORAL LOBES.

WHICH WOULD IMPAIR HIS VISION AND MEMORY, RESPECTIVELY.

HEY, CHECK THIS OUT!

SOME PEOPLE WITH TRAUMATIC BRAIN INJURY CAN SUDDENLY DEVELOP A WHOLE NEW TALENT!

OFTEN FOR MUSIC OR ART.

THAT SOUNDS PRETTY FANTASTIC!

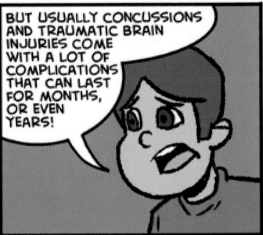

BUT USUALLY CONCUSSIONS AND TRAUMATIC BRAIN INJURIES COME WITH A LOT OF COMPLICATIONS THAT CAN LAST FOR MONTHS, OR EVEN YEARS!

THAT SOUNDS ROUGH. I GUESS GREG REALLY DOES NEED OUR HELP. BUT WHAT CAN WE DO? HE MUST HAVE ALREADY GONE TO THE DOCTOR, TO GET THOSE CRUTCHES AND SUPER-THICK GLASSES.

BUT HE WAS TOO EMBARRASSED TO SHOW HIS GLASSES TO ANYONE! AND HE WAS REALLY BUMMED THAT HE'S NOT ALLOWED TO PLAY SPORTS, EITHER. HE MUST BE FEELING SO SAD AND ALONE.

I HAVE AN IDEA!

THE NEXT DAY...

132

I'M SORRY I'M LATE AGAIN, MS. Z. I JUST HAD THE WORST HEADACHE THIS MORNING. YOU PROBABLY THINK I'M MAKING IT UP, BUT I PROMISE I'M NOT! THE DOCTOR SAYS I NEED TO KEEP WEARING MY—

IT'S ALL RIGHT, GREG. I UNDERSTAND.

YOU—YOU DO?

WHOA. WHAT'S GOING ON?

WE FIGURED OUT WHAT YOU'RE GOING THROUGH, GREG, AND WE'RE REALLY SORRY THAT'S HAPPENING TO YOU.

WE DIDN'T WANT YOU TO FEEL ALONE...

...OR EMBARRASSED ABOUT YOUR NEW GLASSES!

SO WE MADE SOME FOR EVERYBODY!

REAL ABILITIES

CREATED BY: NAVA R. SILTON, PH.D.

ILLUSTRATED BY CHRISTOPHER GOMEZ

MEET THE **REAL ABILITIES** TEAM!

UNO

RJ

SEEMORE

EZRA

MELODY

ADDY

REALABILITIES "CHESSMATES"

ROSALIA

ANIBEL

CREATED BY: NAVA R. SILTON, PH.D.
LEAD AUTHORS: NAVA R. SILTON, PH.D. & MICHAL RICHARDSON
ILLUSTRATOR: CHRISTOPHER GOMEZ
ANIMATION DESIGN: CHRISTOPHER GOMEZ AND MICHAEL SCANLON
RESEARCH TEAM: NAVA SILTON, REGINA COLIE, PATRICK RILEY, AND DINA ZUCKERBERG (MYFACE).

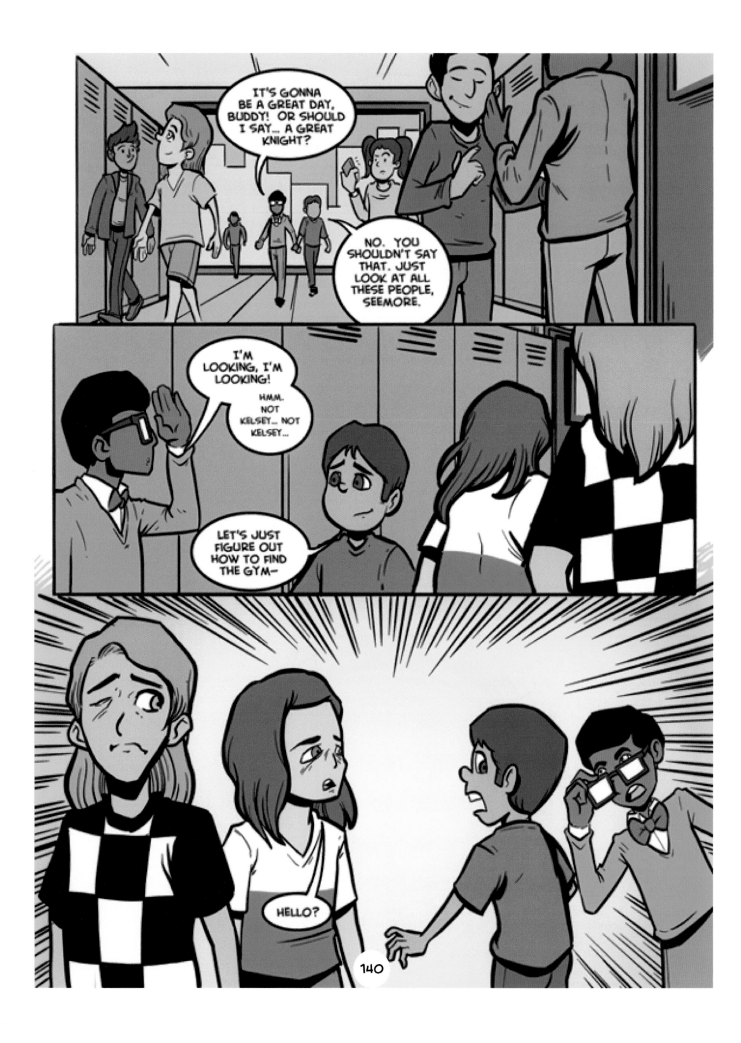

OH, UM, HI, UH--

YOU'RE STARING AT US.

WE MAY LOOK A BIT DIFFERENT. BUT WE'RE JUST REGULAR KIDS, LIKE YOU GUYS. SO INSTEAD OF STARING, JUST COME SAY HI AND IF YOU HAVE QUESTIONS, JUST ASK.

OH SO SORRY, WE DIDN'T MEAN TO STARE.

YES, WE TOTALLY APOLOGIZE. IT'S NICE TO MEET YOU BOTH.

THANKS FOR SAYING THAT. I'M ANIBEL. THIS IS ROSALIA.

I'M SEEMORE, AND THIS IS UNO. UM, SO WE'RE LOOKING FOR KEL--

THE GYM. WE'RE LOOK-ING FOR THE GYM.

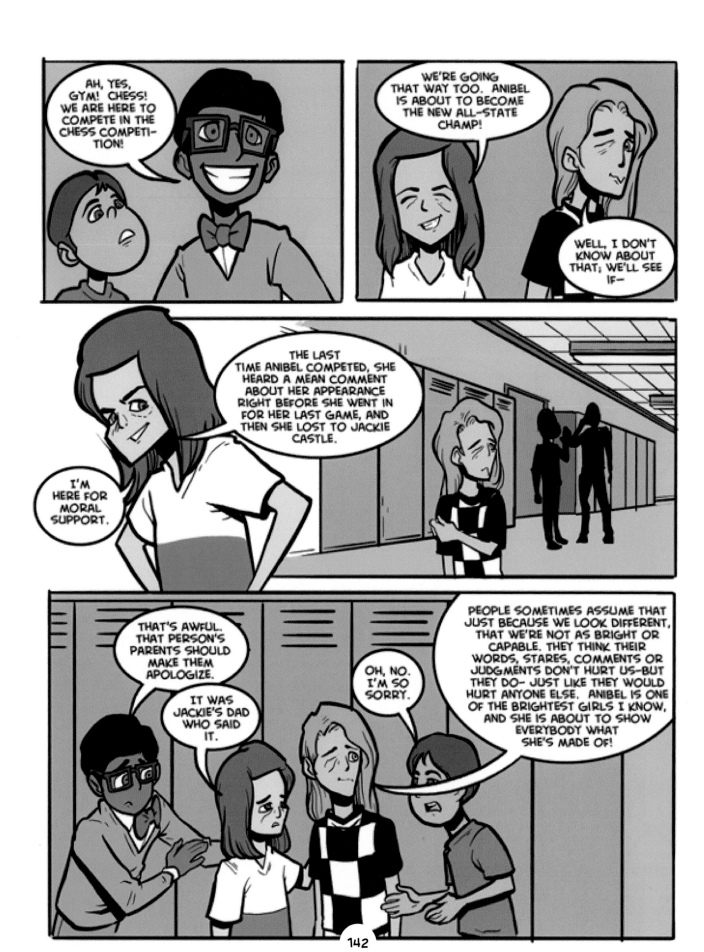

142

143

SEEMORE!

KELSEY! I'M SO HAPPY TO SEE YOU!

I DIDN'T KNOW YOU PLAYED CHESS. BUT I WAS SO HAPPY TO SEE YOUR NAME IN THE TOURNAMENT! I WANT YOU TO MEET MY FRIEND ROSALIA. SHE GOES TO SCHOOL WITH ME HERE.

OH, YES, ROSALIA.

WE'VE MET. AND YOU REMEMBER ANIBEL.

YES, YES, OF COURSE.

I KEEP THINKING ABOUT WHAT YOU SAID EARLIER. ABOUT A GROWN-UP BULLYING ANIBEL.

IT CAN BE HARD TO LOOK DIFFERENT. PEOPLE DON'T ALWAYS KNOW WHAT TO SAY OR DO WHEN THEY SEE ME. AND SOMETIMES I JUST KNOW THAT THEY ARE THINKING OR ABOUT TO SAY SOMETHING UNKIND.

I JUST TRY TO BE KIND. I THINK MOST PEOPLE WANT TO BE KIND, TOO. THEY'RE JUST A LITTLE CONFUSED WHEN THEY SEE SOMETHING DIFFERENT. AND FACES CAN FEEL VERY PERSONAL TO PEOPLE.

146

THE HUMAN BRAIN LOVES FACES. EVEN INFANTS PREFER THE PATTERN OF A FACE TO ANY OTHER GEOMETRIC PATTERN.

THAT'S TRUE. SO WHEN WE SEE A FACE THAT DOESN'T LOOK LIKE WHAT WE'RE USED TO, IT CAN MAKE SOME PEOPLE FEEL LIKE SOMETHING'S NOT RIGHT —

AND THAT CAN MAKE THEM FEEL NERVOUS OR UNCOMFORTABLE.

SO THEY'LL LOOK AT SOMEONE DIFFERENT AND THINK, "SOMETHING FEELS OFF."

OR THEY'LL THINK, "THIS PERSON DOESN'T LOOK 'USUAL' — SO IT'S OKAY TO STARE AT HIM/HER, OR PRETEND HE/SHE DOESN'T EXIST, OR ASSUME HE/SHE DOESN'T HAVE A MIND AND FEELINGS, JUST LIKE EVERYBODY ELSE." IT CAN FEEL REALLY LONELY AND UPSETTING SOMETIMES.

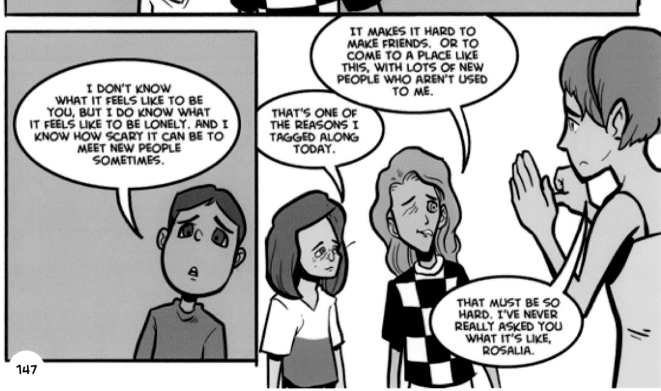

I DON'T KNOW WHAT IT FEELS LIKE TO BE YOU, BUT I DO KNOW WHAT IT FEELS LIKE TO BE LONELY. AND I KNOW HOW SCARY IT CAN BE TO MEET NEW PEOPLE SOMETIMES.

IT MAKES IT HARD TO MAKE FRIENDS. OR TO COME TO A PLACE LIKE THIS, WITH LOTS OF NEW PEOPLE WHO AREN'T USED TO ME.

THAT'S ONE OF THE REASONS I TAGGED ALONG TODAY.

THAT MUST BE SO HARD. I'VE NEVER REALLY ASKED YOU WHAT IT'S LIKE, ROSALIA.

WELL YOU'RE A SUPER-SENSITIVE AND SWEET PERSON, KELSEY! I CAN'T TELL YOU THE NUMBER OF TIMES PEOPLE HAVE ASKED ME, "WHAT HAPPENED TO YOUR FACE," OR "WHY DON'T YOU GET IT FIXED?" I WAS BORN WITH GOLDENHAR SYNDROME, WHICH COMES WITH LOTS OF COMPLICATIONS. IT CAN AFFECT YOUR EAR, NOSE, SOFT PALATE, LIP, JAW, ETC. THAT'S ACTUALLY WHY I GO TO MELLBROOK, SINCE I HAVE A HEARING IMPAIRMENT ASSOCIATED WITH THE SYNDROME. I'VE ALREADY HAD HALF A DOZEN SURGERIES TO HELP MAKE MY LIFE A LITTLE EASIER, BUT IT'S NEVER GOING TO BE "FIXED." IT'S JUST SOMETHING I HAVE TO LIVE WITH.

I ALSO HAVE PROPORTIONATE DWARFISM, WHICH MEANS I AM SMALLER THAN AVERAGE, DUE TO A GROWTH HORMONE DEFICIENCY. SOME OF MY FRIENDS HAVE A DISPROPORTIONATE FORM OF DWARFISM, CALLED ACHONDROPLASIA. WE MIGHT BE SHORTER, BUT WE SURE HAVE BIG DREAMS AND ABILITIES, LIKE EVERYONE ELSE.

IF PEOPLE ASK ME ABOUT IT, I'M HAPPY TO EXPLAIN TO THEM ABOUT MY TREACHER COLLINS SYNDROME (TCS). TREACHER COLLINS IS A GENETIC DISORDER AND IT USUALLY AFFECTS THE EARS, EYES, CHEEKBONES AND CHIN. PEOPLE CAN HAVE MILD OR MORE SEVERE FORMS. SOMETIMES PEOPLE HAVE BREATHING PROBLEMS, HAVE DIFFICULTY SEEING AND HEARING AND THEY MAY HAVE A CLEFT PALATE.

BUT PEOPLE WITH TCS ARE JUST AS INTELLIGENT AS ANYONE ELSE, LIKE MY BRILLIANT FRIEND HERE, ANIBEL! SO PEOPLE NEED TO STOP STARING OR LOOKING AWAY AND START GETTING TO LEARN THE WONDERFUL THINGS ABOUT ANIBEL AND ABOUT MY OTHER FRIENDS WITH FACIAL DIFFERENCES.

LIKE THIS: HEY, ANIBEL! IT'S NICE TO SEE YOU AGAIN. HOW'S THE CHESS TOURNAMENT GOING?

THANKS FOR ASKING, UNO. IT'S GOING REALLY WELL—I'VE WON EVERY MATCH SO FAR!

WHICH MEANS YOU'LL BE BE PLAYING A TOUGH COMPETITOR FOR YOUR FINAL MATCH!

LAST MATCH, EVERYONE! ANIBEL TORRES TO TABLE TWELVE, PLEASE...

WELL, GOOD LUCK, EVERYONE!

ANIBEL! IT'S SO GOOD TO SEE YOU AGAIN!

GOOD LUCK, ANIBEL...

GOOD LUCK!

THE BELL HAS RUNG. NO TALKING, PLEASE!

GOOD LUCK!

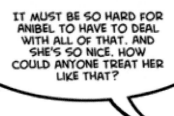

IT MUST BE SO HARD FOR ANIBEL TO HAVE TO DEAL WITH ALL OF THAT. AND SHE'S SO NICE. HOW COULD ANYONE TREAT HER LIKE THAT?

UNO IS SO NICE. AND PRETTY SMART, TOO! BUT THERE'S SOMETHING HE FORGOT...

CHECKMATE!

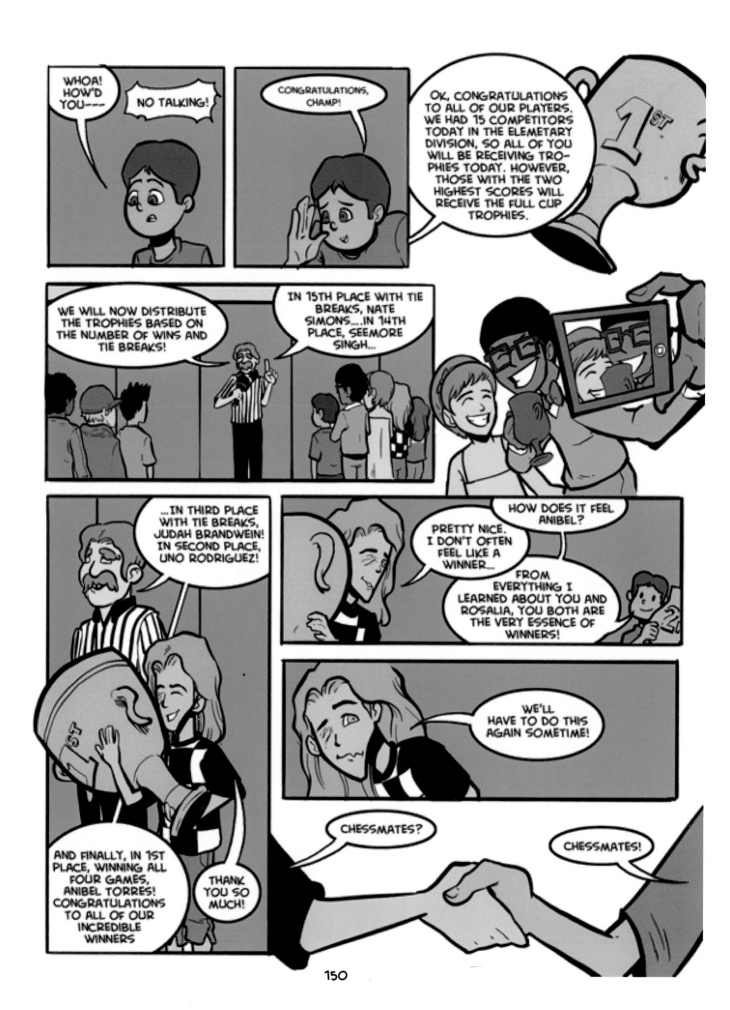

AUTHOR/CREATOR

NAVA R. SILTON, PH.D., A DEVELOPMENTAL PSYCHOLOGIST, RECEIVED HER B.S. FROM CORNELL UNIVERSITY IN 2002 AND HER M.A. AND PH.D. FROM FORDHAM UNIVERSITY IN 2009. SILTON HAS WORKED AT NICKELODEON, SESAME STREET WORKSHOP, MEDIAKIDZ AND HAS CONSULTED FOR NETFLIX AND THE AUTISM SEAVER CENTER. SHE APPEARS REGULARLY ON FOX 5 NEWS AS A PSYCHOLOGICAL CORRESPONDENT AND HAS APPEARED ON NBC NEWS, THE THOM HARTMANN SHOW AND ON VARIOUS RADIO STATIONS. SILTON HAS WRITTEN OVER THREE DOZEN PEER-REVIEWED JOURNAL ARTICLES AND OVER THIRTY ACADEMIC CHAPTERS, BOOK REVIEWS AND ENCYCLOPEDIA ENTRIES. SHE HAS ALSO EDITED SIX FULL TEXTBOOKS. HER FIRST TWO BOOKS DISCUSS INNOVATIVE TECHNOLOGIES FOR INDIVIDUALS WITH AUTISM AND OTHER DISABILITIES, HER THIRD DELVES INTO CREATIVITY, HER FOURTH INTO FAMILY DYNAMICS AND ROMANTIC RELATIONSHIPS, HER FIFTH INTO HAPPINESS, GRATITUDE, KINDNESS, EMPATHY AND WELL-BEING AND HER SIXTH INTO BEST CHILD DEVELOPMENT AND PARENTING PRACTICES FOR THE TWENTY-FIRST CENTURY.

SILTON CREATED THE REALABILITIES EDUCATIONAL COMIC BOOK SERIES CURRICULUM (WWW.REALABILITIES.COM), WHICH OFFERS 15 COMICS (12 RELATED TO DISABILITIES AND 3 RELATED TO MENTAL HEALTH DISORDERS) AND TWO INSTRUCTIONAL MANUALS FOR USE IN CLASSROOMS ACROSS THE WORLD. THE REALABILITIES COMIC BOOK SERIES HAS NOW BEEN TRANSLATED INTO SPANISH, HEBREW, FRENCH AND CHINESE. DUE TO THE POPULARITY OF THE REALABILITIES SERIES IN THE SCHOOLS, SILTON CREATED ADDY & UNO, THE FIRST FAMILY MUSICAL ABOUT DISABILITIES, BULLYING AND KINDNESS. MOST RECENTLY, ADDY & UNO RAN FOR 18 MONTHS OFF-BROADWAY AT THEATER ROW ON 42ND STREET IN NEW YORK, NY AND IS CURRENTLY TRAVELING TO SCHOOLS ALL ACROSS THE TRISTATE AREA AND BEYOND. REALABILITIES AND ADDY & UNO INTEND TO FILL A SIGNIFICANT VOID IN CHILDREN'S LITERATURE AND MEDIA, SO THAT INDIVIDUALS WITH DISABILITIES AND MENTAL HEALTH DISORDERS CAN SEE THEMSELVES REPRESENTED POSITIVELY ON-SCREEN AND TYPICAL CHILDREN AND ADULTS CAN BECOME INCREASINGLY KNOWLEDGEABLE, SENSITIVE AND INTERESTED IN THEIR PEERS WITH DISABILITIES AND/OR MENTAL HEALTH DISORDERS. MOREOVER, THE COMIC SERIES AND SHOW SEEK TO PROMOTE A STOP BULLYING PLATFORM. SILTON IS MARRIED TO DR. ARIEL BRANDWEIN AND HAS THREE LITTLE MEN AND TWO LITTLE LADIES!

CHRISTOPHER GOMEZ IS A CARTOONIST AND ILLUSTRATOR WHO SPECIALIZES IN MAINSTREAM COMICS GEARED TOWARDS YOUTH AND YOUNG ADULTS. WITH TRAINING IN BOTH COMPUTER TECHNOLOGY AND FINE ARTS, HE POSSESSES ABILITY IN BOTH TRADITIONAL AND DIGITAL MEDIUMS. HE GRADUATED WITH A DEGREE IN CARTOONING FROM THE SCHOOL OF VISUAL ARTS AND IS OUR PRIMARY COMIC BOOK ILLUSTRATOR. HIS PERSONAL WEBSITE IS: CHRISGOMEZART.COM. YOU CAN SEE HIS PORTFOLIO AT- HTTP://PORTFOLIOS.SVA.EDU/CHRISGOMEZART

FORMATTING BY ANTHONY J. INGARGIOLA

FOR MORE INFORMATION, PLEASE VISIT OUR WEBSITE: WWW.REALABILITIES.COM
TO CONTACT DR. NAVA SILTON DIRECTLY: NAVA.SILTON@GMAIL.COM